EARTHWISE

Our Planet

Pam Robson

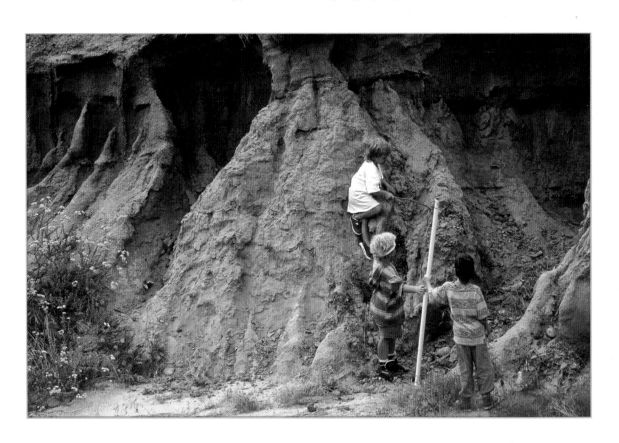

Franklin Watts
London • Sydney

CONTENTS

PAPERBACK EDITION PRINTED 2008

© Aladdin Books Ltd 2004

Designed and produced by
Aladdin Books Ltd
2/3 Fitzroy Mews
London W1T 6DF

First published in 2004 by
Franklin Watts
338 Euston Road
London NW1 3BH

Franklin Watts Australia
Level 17/207 Kent Street
Sydney NSW 2000

Franklin Watts is a division
of Hachette Children's Books

Editor: Jim Pipe

Educational Consultant:
Jackie Holderness

Series Design: Flick, Book
Design and Graphics

Designer: Simon Morse

Picture Research: Brian Smart

ISBN 978 0 7496 8141 8

A catalogue record for this
book is available from the
British Library.

Dewey Classification: 551

Printed in Malaysia

INTRODUCTION

We live on a rocky planet called Earth. Its surface, the land, is changing all the time. Earthquakes split the ground and volcanoes create new mountains. Wind and water slowly wear away the land. People can also change the land. They dam rivers and tunnel through mountains.

HOW TO USE THIS BOOK

Look for the symbol of the magnifying glass for tips on looking at the landscape in your area.

The paintbrush boxes contain activities that relate to the shape of the land where you live.

OUR PLANET

From space, our planet looks smooth. But on the ground we can see hills, valleys and cliffs. All of these make up the surface of the Earth – what we call the landscape.

Salty seas and oceans cover much of Earth's surface. Under the water are mountains, hills and valleys that we cannot see. We only see the shape of the land that is above water.

Using a Map

Look at maps of the area where you live. Is the landscape flat or hilly? Lines called contours show the height of the land above sea level. Take a walk near your home and see if you can spot the hills on the map. Where contour lines are very close together the hill will be steep.

EARTH

Our planet is a huge rock spinning in space. But when you dig down into the ground, you will find that much of Earth's rocky surface is covered by a layer of soil in which trees and other plants grow.

Soil is made up of tiny pieces of rock. These contain the minerals that plants need to grow. Soil also contains air, water and rotting plant and animal matter. Another word for soil is earth – which gives us the name for our planet!

From space, Earth looks like a shining blue ball because there is so much water on its surface. Clouds swirl around in the atmosphere. The atmosphere is the layer of air that surrounds our planet. Without air, water and energy from the Sun, there would be no life on Earth.

Hills and Valleys – Rivers flow through valleys between hills. The tallest hills are mountains.

Coasts – Where the land meets the sea there may be high cliffs or sandy beaches.

Lowlands and Plains – A flat, gentle landscape often has good soil for farming.

INSIDE THE EARTH

We can see what is on Earth's surface. But if you could dig a hole down to Earth's centre, what would you find? No one knows for sure. Scientists try to find out by exploring its different layers. They study rocks, earthquakes and volcanoes (below).

If Earth could be sliced open, it would be like a giant peach. Its skin, the Earth's surface, is called the crust. Below this is the mantle, a layer of hot, sticky rock. Earth's centre is called the core. The outer core is red-hot liquid rock, called magma. The inner core is made of solid nickel and iron. It is 100 times hotter than the hottest desert!

Crust
Mantle
Outer core
Inner core

Giant pieces of Earth's crust move around on top of the soft mantle beneath. These moving pieces of crust are called tectonic plates.

When these giant plates push against each other, earthquakes can shake the ground, volcanoes can erupt and mountains may slowly form.

World Jigsaw

Find a world map in an atlas. Photocopy the map and glue it on to cardboard. Cut out the continents of Africa and South America. They almost fit together like jigsaw pieces, because they were once joined together.

Africa

South America

The San Andreas Fault (above) is the place where two tectonic plates meet beneath the US state of California. When one of the plates slips suddenly, it can cause an earthquake in the cities of Los Angeles or San Francisco.

A very long time ago the continents were close together in one large piece of land called Pangaea. Over millions of years the tectonic plates have moved apart. The continents are now separate chunks of land.

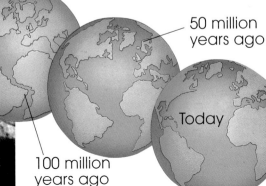

200 million years ago

Pangaea

50 million years ago

Today

100 million years ago

ROCKS

Rock is the hard, solid part of Earth's crust. There are many types of rock, which people use in different ways. Granite is a hard rock used in building. It is a type of **igneous** rock. This means it formed when magma from below the ground cooled on the surface. Other rocks, such as marble, form when they are squeezed and pushed deep below the ground. We call them **metamorphic** rocks.

Rockface

Fossil

Some rocks are made of materials that were once part of older rocks. Small pieces of rock form layers of sand and mud on the seabed. Over millions of years, the layers turn into a rock we call **sedimentary** rock. When dead plants and animals get buried in layers of sand and mud, they can leave shapes in the rock as it forms. These are known as fossils.

ROCKFACES

Look at cliffs (left) and road cuttings. You may see layers of rock, called strata. Can you spot any faults, places where layers of rock break? Imagine how the rocks are slowly forced up and down by movements inside the Earth.

Rock Collection

Pebbles

Chalk

Different rocks are made up of different mixtures of minerals. Some minerals form gemstones, such as rubies, inside the rock. Find out more by making your own collection. Test each sample. Is it very hard? Or does it easily crumble like chalk? Does it feel rough or smooth? You can also use a spotter's book to find out the names of your rocks.

The Rock Cycle

Hard rock forms when magma from below the ground cools. This rock is worn away and the grains become sand or mud. These form sedimentary rock. This is forced beneath the surface where it changes again. This new rock is pushed up as magma or as a mountain. Then the rock cycle begins again.

Grains of rock form mud or sand (deposition).

Rock is worn away by weather (erosion).

Igneous rock forms when hot, liquid rock (magma) is pushed to the surface.

Layers of sand form **sedimentary rock**. This is forced underground.

CHANGING LANDSCAPES

Every hill, cliff or river near you is always changing. Rocks and soil are worn away by wind, rain, ice, rivers and waves. This is called erosion. Then the grains of rock are carried to a different place by rivers and streams. This is called deposition.

Mountain tops are shaped by ice.

Cracking Clay

Do your own experiment to see how ice splits rock into smaller pieces. Spray two balls of clay with water. Then wrap them in cling film. Place one ball in the freezer for a day. Then take it out and allow the ice to melt. Repeat this a few more times. Cracks will appear in the frozen clay. But the ball outside the freezer will be unchanged.

Crack

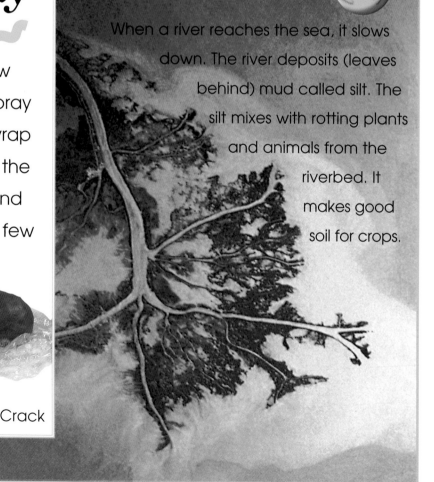

When a river reaches the sea, it slows down. The river deposits (leaves behind) mud called silt. The silt mixes with rotting plants and animals from the riverbed. It makes good soil for crops.

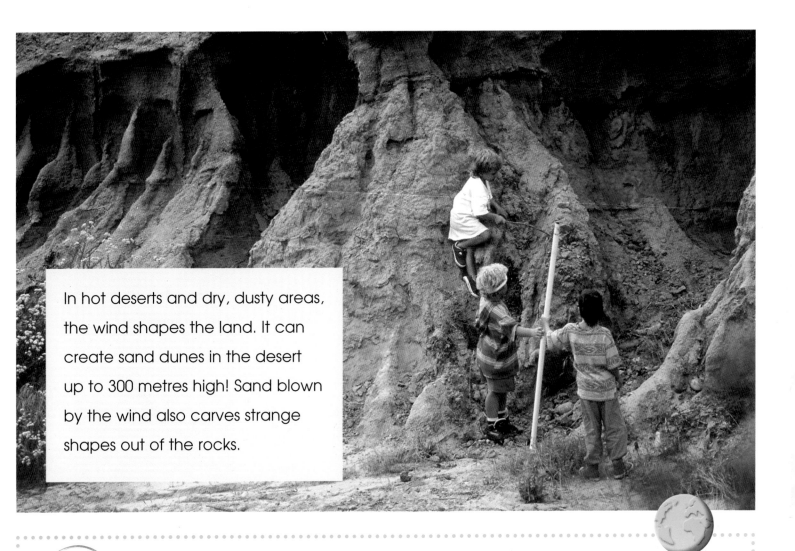

In hot deserts and dry, dusty areas, the wind shapes the land. It can create sand dunes in the desert up to 300 metres high! Sand blown by the wind also carves strange shapes out of the rocks.

WEARING • AWAY • BUILDINGS

Look at the outside of your house or school. Can you see where the weather is wearing away the stone or brick? Look also for rotting wood, flaky paint or rusty metal. This erosion takes many years. But car and lorry fumes add chemicals to the rain. This causes acid rain, which wears away buildings faster.

MOUNTAINS

Have you ever seen a long line of mountains? This is called a mountain range. Mountain ranges are created by huge forces under the ground. Some are made by volcanoes. Other mountains form when tectonic plates bump into each other. They are like giant "wrinkles" in the rocks.

Mountain Scenes

Mountains are very beautiful, so many artists like to paint mountain scenes. J.M.W. Turner painted this stunning picture of the Alps. Paint your own picture of a mountain scene. Try to show how high your mountain is by painting the clouds at the top of the mountain.

In countries like Portugal (above) farmers grow crops even on mountain slopes. A series of level steps is built around the slope. Each step, or terrace, is separated from the next by a wall. This stops water from running down the slope.

Mountain climbers enjoy trying to reach the top of a mountain, called the summit. As you go up a mountain, it becomes colder and there is less air to breathe. Some mountain tops are so high they are covered in snow all year round.

Hotels and resorts are built in snow-covered mountain regions. Tourists travel on special railways that can travel up steep mountain slopes. Cable cars carry skiers to the top of the mountain. People slide down the slopes on snowboards (above) or skis.

Engineers build tunnels through mountains for roads and railways. They use explosives to blow holes in the rock. Then machines take away the rock pieces. Tunnels make journeys shorter and faster. One of the longest railway tunnels is the Simplon Tunnel in the Alps, which is 20 kilometres long.

When a volcano is likely to erupt, we say that it is active. For example, Mount Etna on the island of Sicily erupts regularly. Mount Fuji in Japan (right) has not erupted for a very long time. We say that it is dormant.

VOLCANOES

A volcano is a hole in the Earth's crust. Hot liquid rock from deep below the ground forces itself through the crack. The volcano erupts (bursts out). It can shoot ash, gas or hot rock high into the air. After many eruptions, a volcanic mountain may form.

RING • OF • FIRE

Volcanoes often occur where two tectonic plates meet. Look in an atlas to locate Earth's "Ring of Fire" volcanoes (right). They are found in a ring around the edge of the Pacific Ocean. Their cone-shaped peaks stick out above the water. Other volcanoes to look for are Mount St. Helens in the United States, Stromboli and Vesuvius in Italy and Pinatubo in the Philippines.

Ring of Fire

▲ Active volcano

Another group of volcanoes lies in the Atlantic Ocean. The island of Surtsey rose from the sea after one of these volcanoes erupted in 1963.

Mount Kilimanjaro in Tanzania is Africa's highest mountain. It is an extinct volcano. This means that it will never erupt again.

EARTHQUAKES

If you stand up on a moving bus, it can feel like the floor is wobbling. When an earthquake happens, the ground below shakes. Most earthquakes happen in places where tectonic plates meet.

When a tectonic plate moves suddenly, it causes huge vibrations in the ground. We call this an earthquake. It can make trees, buildings and bridges fall down.

An earthquake's energy is measured using the Richter scale. Many old buildings collapse when an earthquake is 7.5 or more on the Richter scale. But buildings can now be built to withstand almost any earthquake.

MOVING • EARTH

After an earthquake the shape of the land is changed. Huge cracks appear in the ground (left). Rocks split open. You may see signs of smaller earth movements in your area. If you live near a cliff, you may see the effect of a landslide. Rocks, soil and trees slide down the hill.

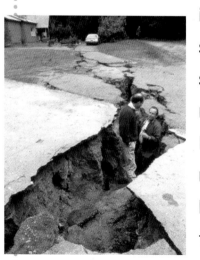

Weak spots in the Earth's crust are known as fault lines (page 7). These happen where tectonic plates meet. Places near fault lines, such as Turkey and Iran, are more likely to have earthquakes.

Make an Earthquake

Lay a pencil on the table in front of you. Push hard down and forward on the table. Then allow your hand to slip forward suddenly. This creates vibrations, like an earthquake, making the pencil shake.

RIVER JOURNEY

Rivers also shape the landscape around you. See how channels form if you trickle water from the top of a mound of sand. Rivers usually begin in the hills or mountains. Some rivers begin as melting water from a river of ice called a glacier. Others begin as springs that bubble out of the ground.

A stream rushes downhill. It cuts a narrow valley with steep sides. This is in the shape of the letter "V".

Waterfalls form when soft rock is worn away.

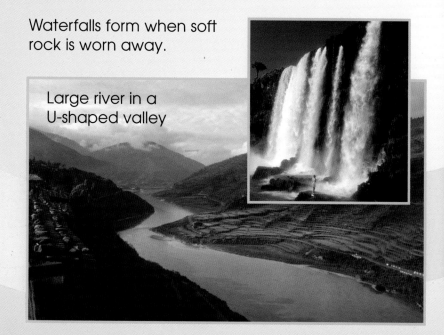

Large river in a U-shaped valley

Sticks Game

See how the water flows fastest on the outside of a river bend. Play a game by dropping sticks into a stream. Observe the path taken by each stick. What happens on the bends? Does the water move faster?

DO NOT GO NEAR WATER WITHOUT AN ADULT.

As it flows downhill, a stream is joined by rainwater and water from other streams. It becomes a wide river and slows down. The river wears away the valley sides. This makes the valley the shape of a letter "U".

SPRING • WATER

Look in your local supermarket for bottles of spring water. Read the labels to find out where the water comes from. Why do you think spring water is good for you? Think of the minerals the water picks up as it flows over rocks.

The river bends get larger.

By the time a river reaches the sea, it is very wide and moves very slowly. All the silt carried in the river is deposited close to the river mouth. Silt from a large river may form a delta where the river joins the sea. Silt makes good soil for growing crops such as rice.

As the river gets closer to the sea, the bends get larger. On the inside of each bend the water flows so slowly that silt (mud) is deposited. On the outside of a bend it wears away the river bank.

The river reaches the sea.

CAVES AND CAVERNS

DO NOT ENTER CAVES WITHOUT AN ADULT

Below our feet is a dark, damp landscape we rarely see. Limestone rock has lots of cracks which allow rainwater to seep (leak) through the rock. Over millions of years, the water wears away the rock. It can form networks of caves and passages. Amazing stalactites hang from cave ceilings. Stalagmites point upwards from the floor.

CAVE • VISIT

Look at a map of your local area. Are there any caves in your area that are open to visitors?

In many parts of the world, you can visit spectacular caves. Many caves have underground lakes, rivers, and waterfalls. Paths and electric lights allow visitors to explore the caves safely.

Stalagmites

Thousands of years ago, caves were used as homes. Wall paintings have been found on the walls of caves in Lascaux, France. They show how people lived at that time. There are pictures of cows and horses (left).

Stalactites

The longest cave ever to be explored is the Mammoth-Flint Ridge cave system in Kentucky. Explorers have mapped almost 550 kilometres of caves and passageways.

Amazing Shapes

When rainwater flows over limestone, tiny pieces of rock mix into the water, or "dissolve". When the water dries up, it leaves the pieces of rock behind. Over a very long time, these build up into stalactites. Grow your own stalactite using washing soda, which also dissolves in water. Fill two jars with the solution (mix). Place a length of wool between the jars. Dip its ends in the solution.

COASTS

The chemicals in salty sea water dissolve rocks like limestone and chalk. Huge cliffs are slowly dissolved by the waves. Many tourists like to visit the gigantic rock shapes carved by the sea.

DO NOT GO NEAR THE EDGE OF A CLIFF

If you are walking on a beach, look out for amazing cliff scenery. Steep cliffs are shaped into curved arches. Single rock stacks rise from the sea. Day after day, the power of the waves slowly changes the shape of our coasts. Rocks are worn away; cliffs fall into the sea. Three weapons attack the land – water (waves), air (wind) and stone (pebbles).

Shipwrecked!

Rocky coasts are dangerous places for ships caught in a storm. Imagine being on board a huge sailing ship that is shipwrecked in a violent storm. Write your own shipwreck story. Think about the howling wind and giant waves crashing on the shore.

PROTECTING • THE • COAST

Next time you visit the seashore, look around and see what is being done to protect the coast. Concrete and boulders stop waves from crashing onto the shore (right). Barriers called groynes stop waves from sweeping sand off sandy beaches.

Rubbing sandpaper on wood makes it smooth. When waves fling pebbles and sand against the cliffs, it works in the same way. Slowly the cliffs are worn away. Pebbles become rounded because they rub against each other.

Arch

Headland

Waves crash against a headland where a cliff sticks out into the sea. The waves carve out two caves, one in each side of the headland. Waves then crash inside the caves until only an arch of rock is left. Eventually, the arch collapses. Only a stack is left.

SEASHORE

A sandy beach is a fun place to be, but not all beaches are sandy. There are rocky, pebble and muddy beaches. Sand is made from tiny pieces of rock worn away from cliffs. Waves carry sand to a sheltered place on the coast. This is often a bay between two rocky headlands.

Visitors to many European beaches can now see huge offshore wind turbines (top). Sea breezes keep the turbines turning, producing electricity.

Sandy beach

Rocky beach

Huge oil tankers travel the seas carrying oil from country to country. However, oil from shipwrecked tankers has damaged the wildlife of many coastlines. Oil spills (left) cause pollution that kills many sea animals and plants. Dead sea birds, fish and sea mammals are washed up on the shore.

Pebble beach

Have you ever been to the seaside for a holiday? Beaches all over the world have become holiday resorts. A lot of money is spent keeping the resorts free of pollution and litter.

Collecting Pebbles

A pebble beach is a good place to find different rocks. Walk along the beach after the tide has gone out. Collect different pebbles. Choose a large pebble from your collection to decorate with paint.

UNDER THE SEA

Imagine if Earth's oceans drained away. You would see mountains and valleys just as there are on land. Scientists look at the sea bed using deep-sea craft called submersibles. The deepest parts of the ocean are valleys called trenches. Some trenches are nearly 11 kilometres deep. An extinct volcano, Mauna Kea, is taller than the tallest mountain on land, Mount Everest. It measures 10 kilometres from the ocean floor.

Much of Earth's oil and gas has been found beneath the sea. It is buried in layers of sedimentary rock. Offshore platforms (left) have been built to pump oil and gas from the sea bed.

Near the shore, the land slopes gently down. This part of the seabed is the continental shelf. Then the seabed falls steeply, like a giant cliff.

A huge flat plain covers half of the ocean floor. A line of mountains runs along the middle of the ocean. This is the mid-ocean ridge.

Plain

Ridge

Trench

Shelf

Seamounts (mountains)

Volcanoes

CORAL • REEFS

Coral reefs are a very colourful part of the ocean. Reefs are found in warm, shallow seas close to shore. They provide homes and food for many plants and animals. If you can, watch one of the many TV programmes about reefs. Learn about the fish, crabs, turtles and other animals that live on a coral reef.

Scientists have found tall volcanic chimneys (above) on the ocean floor. The chimneys are called Black Smokers because they belch out hot black fumes. These make the water very hot. Only a few animals, like this crab, can live in the hot, poisonous water nearby.

Fossil fuels like coal, oil and gas have been used by people for a long time. Smoke from these fuels has polluted the air. This traps heat from the Sun and may be why the Earth is getting warmer.

DAMAGED LANDSCAPE

People make huge changes to the shape of the land. They dig deep mines and quarries. They build high dams across rivers. They tunnel deep into mountains. Forests are cut down and rubbish is buried under the ground. Our pollution is changing the Earth's climate. Desert areas are spreading and sea levels are rising.

RUBBISH • DUMPS

You probably don't have to look very hard to find rubbish in your area. People produce lots of it! Some rubbish is buried under the ground in places called landfills. But rubbish is also put in open dumps. These dumps can ruin the natural beauty of the landscape.

Litter ruins any landscape (right), including your local streets!

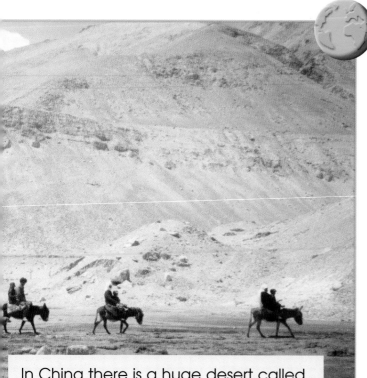

In China there is a huge desert called the Gobi Desert. This desert has been growing bigger every year. One reason for this is that people have cut down forests nearby. To protect the city of Beijing from Gobi sandstorms, trees have been planted close to the city.

When people cut down forests it makes a big change to the landscape. When there are no trees, the soil is easily washed away by rain and wind.

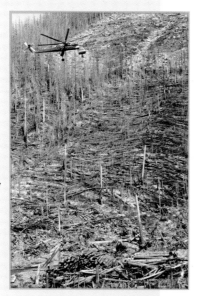

Take Action

Are you worried about your local landscape? Perhaps there are plans to build a road through an ancient forest. Ask your teacher or parent to help you write a letter to your local council. Explain why you enjoy the landscape as it is.

Dams have been built across many large rivers. They use the power of falling water to make electricity. When a dam is built, it creates a lake behind it. This changes the shape of the land forever. Dams can destroy animal homes. People may also be forced to leave their homes.

USEFUL WORDS

atmosphere – the thick layer of air that surrounds Earth.

contours – lines drawn on a map that join places the same height above sea level.

delta – land at the place where a large river enters the sea, formed by silt from the river.

deposition – when grains of rock are carried to a different place by rivers and streams.

dissolve – to make something liquid, often by putting it into liquid. Sugar dissolves in hot water.

Earth's core – the solid metal centre of our planet.

Earth's crust – the rocky outer surface of Earth.

erosion – the wearing away of the land by natural forces such as wind or rain.

fault – a break in Earth's crust, where rocks are pushed up or down.

fossil – (left) the rocky remains or traces of an ancient animal or plant.

groyne – a barrier built across a beach to stop sand or stones from moving.

landscape – our view of the land.

magma – (right) hot, liquid rock from below the Earth's crust.

mantle – the part of Earth below the crust and outside the core.

silt – the fine mud that settles at the bottom of rivers. It is made up of tiny pieces of rock.

soil – a mix of minerals, tiny pieces of rock, dead plant and animal matter, and air and water.

stalactites/stalagmites – the icicle shapes formed when limestone dissolves in rainwater. Stalactites hang from the roof of caves, stalagmites grow from the floor.

tectonic plates – giant pieces of Earth's crust. They move around on top of the soft mantle below.

Find Out More

Take a look at these books & websites:

Books: Volcanoes (Franklin Watts); Geography for Fun: Mountains and Our Moving Earth (Franklin Watts); How the Earth Works (Dorling Kindersley).

Websites: http://volcano.und.nodak.edu
http://earthquake.usgs.gov/4kids
http://mineral.galleries.com/default.htm

STORY • TIME

Look out for the many myths and legends that explain the landscape. In Hawaii, some people say that when the volcano Kilauea erupts, it is a sign that the goddess Pele is angry. In Japan, people once believed that earthquakes happened when the big catfish that lived inside the Earth moved about.

INDEX

Photocredits
Abbreviations: l-left, r-right, b-bottom, t-top, c-centre, m-middle
Front cover tl, tr, bl & br, back cover, 2-3, 5bl, 5bm, 5br, 9mlb, 24bl, 28bl, 28br, 29mr, 29bl, 30tr — Photodisc. Front cover c, 27mr — Stockbyte. Front cover inset, 28ml — Comstock. 1, 6bl, 9bl, 10tr, 11t, 13tr, 13ml, 13br, 14-15, 15 both, 31bl, 32b — Digital Stock. 3b, 18mr, 19br, 24c, 24mr — Argentinian Embassy, London. 4-5, 9lmt, 10br, 25tr, 30-31 — Corbis. 7l, 9br — R. E. Wallace; USGS. 7tr — Brand X Pictures. 8-9 — US National Park Service. 9tl, 25l, 27 main, 27bm — NOAA. 9mr, 12-13, 12bl, 12mr, 14t, 18tl, 18br, 20-21, 20bm, 21t, 21ml, 22 both, 23 both, 29tl, 29br — Corel. 10bl, 17bl, 21br — Select Pictures. 11br, 19tr — PBD. 16bl, 16br, 17t — FEMA. 19ml — US Fish & Wildlife Service. 19bm — John Deere. 24tl — Scott Bauer; ARS. 26ml — Brian Moore; USCG.